Dear parents,

Math anxiety. So many of us suffer from it. Yet every day we measure time or distance, look for patterns, estimate, and count. Whether we realize it or not, we are constantly thinking mathematically. And as parents we hope that our children will not succumb to our math prejudices.

We give children a great deal of encouragement when they are learning to count—but the encouragement needn't stop there. Young children love puzzles and riddles, and they eagerly approach problem-solving situations as if they were games. They often see and use a variety of strategies. These are important skills in developing mathematical thinking.

We truly have the power to nurture in our children a long-lasting love for math. We can do this by making a "math connection" to familiar experiences and by supporting our children's natural affinity for the discipline. **Step into Reading® + Math** books can help. Each book combines an age-appropriate math element with an enjoyable reading experience.

Remember—math is not an isolated phenomenon but is woven into the fabric of our lives. The love of math is a lifelong journey. Celebrate that journey with your child!

Colleen DeFoyd
Primary grades math teacher
Scottsdale, Arizona

*For the most magically magical magic souls I know,
Griffin and Chase!—F.M.*

*For my three terrific cousins, Tyler, Colby,
and Carter Scruggs—R.W.*

Author Acknowledgments: *Thanks to Mallory Loehr, Heidi Kilgras, and Shana Corey for believing in me, and especially Mallory for her support, guidance, and collaboration. With many thanks to Roy Goodman, curator of the American Philosophical Society in Philadelphia, for his expertise on the life of Ben Franklin.*

ISBN 0-439-30920-4

12 11 10 9 8 7 6 5 4 3 2 1   1 2 3 4 5 6/0

Printed in the U.S.A.   23

First Scholastic printing, October 2001

Ben Franklin
and the
MAGIC SQUARES

By Frank Murphy
Illustrated by Richard Walz

SCHOLASTIC INC.
New York Toronto London Auckland Sydney
Mexico City New Delhi Hong Kong Buenos Aires

Over 200 years ago, when America was just 13 colonies, there lived a super smart guy. You may have heard of him. His name was Benjamin Franklin. But most people called him Ben.

This story is about how Ben invented magic squares. But first, there are a few things you need to know about this great man . . .

Ben Franklin wasn't smart for nothing. He put his big brain to good use. He was always thinking and writing and inventing cool things—even when he was a kid.

When he was 11 years old, Ben jumped into a lake holding on to a kite.

The kite was pulled by the wind.

Ben was pulled by the kite.

The kite flew a whole mile with Ben holding on tight!

That same year, Ben wanted to swim faster than anyone. So he made flippers for his hands and feet.

They worked!

Flippers, 1717

People still use a version of Ben's flippers today.

As Ben grew older, he kept thinking and writing and inventing. When he was 23, he wrote and printed a newspaper called *The Pennsylvania Gazette*.

People loved it!

The Pennsylvania Gazette, first edition, 1729

When he was 26, Ben wrote and printed a book called *Poor Richard's Almanac.*

An *almanac* is a book of useful information, from weather predictions and advertisements to important dates. Ben's almanacs had even more things in them. There were witty sayings (*witty* means "clever") and fun puzzles (you know what *fun* means).

People still use many of Ben's sayings today!

Early to bed and early to rise makes a man healthy, wealthy, and wise.

An apple a day keeps the doctor away.

When Ben was 36, he invented a special stove. It kept homes warmer than a fire in a fireplace and burned less wood. Everyone was amazed!

Franklin stove, 1742

People still use Franklin stoves today!

Ben never outgrew his love of kites.
When he was 46, he tied a key to a kite
string and . . .

. . . flew the kite in a thunderstorm!

This was *not* a safe thing to do. But Ben *did* find out that lightning was made of electricity.

Experiments with electricity, 1752

And electricity is used today as well!

Once Ben even invented a special rocking chair. It had a fan on top. Ben rocked back and forth and the fan swished this way and that. It really kept the flies off his head!

No one else ever used *this* invention— not in Ben's time and not in ours!

Over the years, Ben also started
America's first library,

The Library Company
of Philadelphia, 1731

America's first fire station,

Union Fire Company, 1736

and America's first hospital, too!

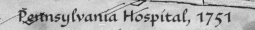

Pennsylvania Hospital, 1751

He even helped Thomas Jefferson write and *re*write the Declaration of Independence in 1776.

To Do

1. Meet with T.J.
2. Fix Kite
3. ~~Invent~~ telephone *maybe later!*
4. Print almanac
5. Make up 5 jokes
6. Play game with William
7. Buy present for Deborah

So you get the idea that Ben Franklin was a super busy guy. Right?

Then you are ready for the story of the magic squares.

It all started in the middle of Ben's life in 1736. That year he became a clerk for the Pennsylvania Colonial Assembly. The *Assembly* was a group of men who made laws for the colony of Pennsylvania. A *clerk* was the person who kept track of all the important decisions they made.

The guys in the Assembly chose Ben
to be a clerk because they knew he was
super smart and a great writer!

Ben listened carefully to the men in the Assembly. He couldn't write anything down until they agreed on something. So Ben waited and waited.

For days, he listened to long arguments about which laws were good and which laws were bad.

For more days, Ben listened to fights about taxes and bills.

And for even *more* days, Ben listened to disagreements about numbers and money, city streets and state laws.

Until one day . . .

The members of the Assembly were not happy.

"Mr. Franklin!" one of them said loudly.

Ben woke up. He was very embarrassed.

"I am so sorry!" he said.

Everyone went back to work.

The men argued.

Ben listened and listened. He kept his ears open and his eyes open. It was very hard.

Day turned into night, and the assemblymen still argued.

Ben found out it was easier to stay
awake if his hands were busy. He twiddled
his thumbs.

He tickled his nose with his quill pen.

He dipped his pen in ink and started to
doodle.

Ben doodled people.

Ben doodled new inventions.

Ben even doodled a doodle of his pet squirrel, Skugg.

The men in the assembly were still arguing. So Ben decided to doodle a math puzzle.

He drew a square. Then he drew two
lines going up and down and two lines
going left and right. This made nine boxes
in one big box.

Ben wrote a different number in each
box.

5	7	3
2	4	9
8	1	6

He stared at the box of numbers. He
waited for an idea to pop into his head.

Ben noticed something! When he added the numbers in the first row, they equaled 15. When he added the numbers in the first column, they equaled 15 as well.

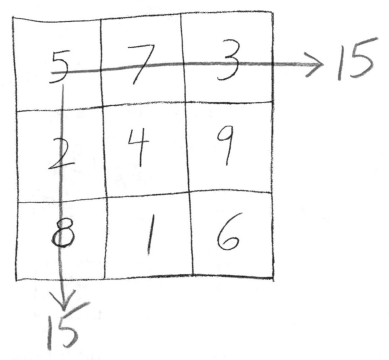

Now Ben wondered if he could make the numbers add up to 15 no matter which row or column he picked. What if they even added up to 15 in a diagonal line? That would be more than a math puzzle, it would be a magic square!

Ben started arranging the numbers . . .

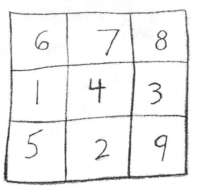

. . . sorting the numbers . . .

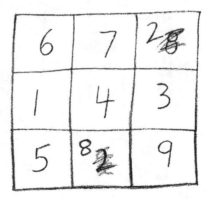

. . . and *re*arranging the numbers!

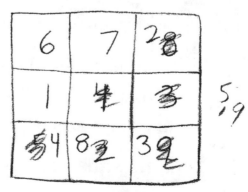

Ben was thinking so hard about his
magic square that he was not sleepy at all!

Finally, he saw what needed to be done!

First he wrote a 1 in the center box of the top row.

Next he wrote a 2 in the last box of the third row.

He wrote a 3 in the first box of the second row.

Then Ben wrote a 4 in the bottom box of the first column. He wrote a 5 in the box in the center. Then a 6 in the third box of the first row.

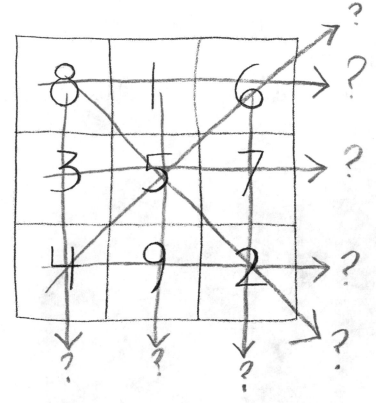

Under the 6, Ben wrote a 7.

Ben wrote an 8 inside the first box of the top row. Finally, he wrote a 9 in the only box left.

Was it a magic square?

Ben started adding.

Each row and column added up to 15.

Even the diagonals added up to 15!

"It's magically magic!" Ben shouted.
He had made a magic square!

After that, Ben never dozed off at the Assembly again.

Instead, he doodled magic squares until either the assemblymen finally made a decision *or* . . .

How about lights on all the streets so people can see at night?

Streetlight bill enacted, 1751. Renewed 1756.

. . . he had a good idea of his own for them!

Ben went on to publish his magic
squares in his newspapers and almanacs.
People loved figuring out the magic
answers.

And they still do!

MAKE YOUR OWN MAGIC SQUARE

A. Draw a square. Draw a tic-tac-toe board inside the square.

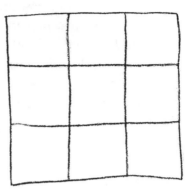

B. Start with the number 1. Put it in the middle of the top row.

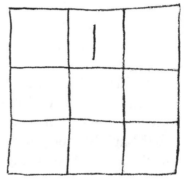

C. Put the number 2 in the box that is directly above and to the right of the 1.

Okay. Wait—hold it! You're probably saying, "There is no box above and to the right of the 1." That's true. So here's what you do: Since there is no box above the 1, drop down to the bottom of the column that holds the 1. *Now* move one square to the right and there you go! Put your number 2 there!

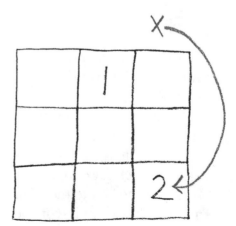

D. Okay, now you're ready for the number 3. So repeat step C: Look for the box above and to the right. Move up one row and then . . . yep, you are correct! There is no box to the right!

What do you do? Move that 3 to the beginning of the row above the 2! Like this!

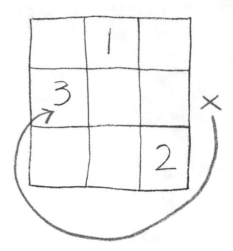

E. Now you are ready for the number 4. Just look above and to the right again!

Yes, you're correct again! There is already a number in the box. So what do you do? Anytime there is a number already in the box you want, just put the next number in the box below the number you just wrote. So put the 4 below the 3.

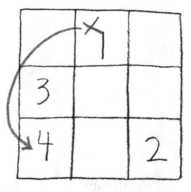

F. Now for the numbers 5 to 9! Always look for the box above and to the right.

If you get stuck, go step by step. If there is no box above, drop down to the bottom of the column, *then* move to the right. If there is no box to the right, move to the beginning of the row. And so on!

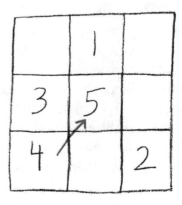

G. Ta-da! Your magic square! What makes it magic? Add the numbers in each of the rows. Now add each of the columns. And finally, add each of the diagonals. What do you get? 15. A perfect magic square!

There are many ways to make magic squares—big ones and little ones! Try starting with 9 and working down to 1! This time, the 9 goes in the middle of the top row, instead of the 1.

8	1	6
3	5	7
4	9	2

AUTHOR'S NOTE

Well, no one knows exactly how or exactly when Ben Franklin came up with magic squares. But we do know these things:

• He really did get bored when he was a clerk in the Pennsylvania Colonial Assembly (1736–1751).

• He definitely made magic squares in 1736 and 1737.

• He called the magic square his "most magically magical magic squares."

• He really invented and made up all the things in this book, plus a lot more!

• He really did have a pet squirrel named Skugg.